Enigma

Selected Poems

Studies in Austrian Literature, Culture and Thought
Translation Series

General Editors:

Jorun B. Johns
Richard H. Lawson

Ingeborg Bachmann

Enigma
Selected Poems

Translated

by

Mike Lyons and Patrick Drysdale

Preface by Heinz Bachmann
Afterword by Hans Höller

Ariadne Press
Riverside, California

Ariadne Press would like to express its appreciation to the Bundesministerium für Unterricht, Kunst und Kultur for assistance in publishing this book.

.KUNST

Translated from the German.
German language copyright © 1978, 2000 by Piper Verlag GmbH, München.
Used with the permission of Zephyr Press, *Darkness Spoken: The Collected Poems*.
www.zephyrpress.org, who control all English language rights.

Library of Congress Cataloging-in-Publication Data

Bachmann, Ingeborg, 1926-1973.
 [Poems. English. Selections]
 Enigma : selected poems / Ingeborg Bachmann ; translated by Mike Lyons and Patrick Drysdale ; afterword by Hans Höller.
     p. cm. -- (Studies in Austrian literature, culture and thought. Translation series)
 ISBN 978-1-57241-181-4 (alk. paper)
 1. Bachmann, Ingeborg, 1926-1973--Translations into English. I. Lyons, Mike. II. Drysdale, Patrick, 1929- III. Title.
 PT2603.A147A2 2011
 831'.914--dc23
                                                    201102599

Cover Design
George McGinnis
Photograph courtesy Heinz Bachmann

Copyright 2011
by Ariadne Press
270 Goins Court
Riverside, CA 92507

All rights reserved.
No part of this publication may be transmitted
in any form or by any means without formal permission.
Printed in the United States of America.
ISBN 978-1-57241-181-4

Contents

From *Poems 1948-1953*	1
Estrangement	2
Drunken Evening	3
Behind the Wall	4
To the Hoof-beat of the Night	5
Spoken to Evening	6
Without People	7
The Harbors Were Opened	8
Still I Fear	9
From *Time on Loan*	11
Outward Voyage	12
Farewell to England	14
Fall Down, Heart	15
Speaking of Darkness	16
Paris	17
Autumn Maneuvers	18
Time on Loan	19
Stars in March	20
In the Twilight	21
Timber and Wood Chips	22
Early Noon	23
Every Day	25
Message	26
Night Flight	27
Psalm	29
In the Deluge of Roses	31

From *Invocation of the Great Bear* — 33
    The Game Is Up — 34
    From About a Land, Its River and Its Lakes — 36
    Invocation of the Great Bear — 38
    My Bird — 39
    Land Settlement — 40
    Curriculum Vitae — 42
    Fog Land — 46
    Explain to Me, Love — 48
    Days in White — 50
    Harlem — 51
    Dead Harbor — 52
    Say and Hearsay — 53
    The First-Born Land — 55
    Songs from an Island — 56
    Roman Nightscape — 60
    Black Waltz — 61
    Shadow Roses Shadow — 62
    Agrigento — 63
    To the Sun — 64
    Songs of Escape — 66

From *Poems 1957-1961* — 75
    Hôtel de la Paix — 76
    Exile — 77
    Miriam — 78
    Current — 79
    Safe Conduct — 80
    You Words — 81

From *Poems 1964-1967*	83
Truly	84
Bohemia Lies on Sea	85
Prague January 64	87
A Kind of Loss	88
Enigma	89
No Frills	90
From *I Know No Better World*	93
My Poems Have Gone Astray	94
I Know No Better World	95
Till Your Return	96
Goodbye	98
Smells	99
The Child	100
Glory Street	101
Farewell	102
The Line of Life	103
Gently, Softly	104
So We Might Die	105
How Difficult Forgiving Is	106
I Lose My Screams	108
Night of Love	109
Wenceslas Square	110
Jewish Cemetery	111
Renunciation	112
Again and Again, Black and White	113
Strangers in the Night	114
Miscellaneous Poems	117
Libraries	118

The Visitor	119
Waiting Room	120
Jacob's Wheel	121
William Turner: Backlight	122
Afterword by Hans Höller	123

Acknowledgments

Acknowledgments are gratefully made to the editors of the following publications, in which some of these translations first appeared: *Dream Catcher, Modern Poetry in Translation, Oxford Magazine, Poetry Review, Stand.*

The translators appreciate the encouragement received from the Austrian Cultural Forum in London, and they are grateful to the friends who have helped with interpretations and suggestions, especially to Karen Leeder of New College, Oxford, to Jim Reed of The Queen's College (now Professor Emeritus), and to David and Helen Constantine, editors of Modern Poetry in Translation, for their early guidance and general helpfulness. They also owe particular thanks to Heinz Bachmann, brother of the poet, for his support and encouragement over several years and to Peter Filkins and Zephyr Press, without whose kind and generous assistance the publication of Enigma could not have come to pass..

Preface

I first met Mike Lyons and Patrick Drysdale some years ago when I attended the British premiere of their translation of Felix Mitterer's *Siberia* at the Unicorn Theatre in Abingdon, Oxfordshire. Impressed by the quality of their translation, I introduced them to Ingeborg's work. They were very enthusiastic and have worked intensively since then to produce this, the first British interpretation since Michael Hamburger's translation in 1967 for *Modern Poetry in Translation*. A contemporary of Ingeborg's, Mike was also responsible for the first translation of her *War Diary*, published by *MPT* in 2008.

From this chance encounter grew lasting friendships and a commitment to my sister's work resulting in the publication of this collection nearly forty years after her death. I believe it will make a valuable contribution to the understanding and appreciation of my sister's poetry.

Heinz Bachmann

From

Poems 1948-1953

Estrangement

Among the trees I can no longer see any trees.
The branches have no leaves to hold them into the wind.
The fruits are sweet but without love.
They don't even satisfy.
So now what is to come?
Before my eyes the forest flees,
before my ear the birds close their mouths,
no meadow serves me as a bed.
I am brimful of time
and hunger for it still.
What is to come?

At night the fires will burn in the mountains.
Shall I set out, approach it all again?

I can no longer see a path in any path.

Drunken Evening

A drunken evening, aglow with boozy light,
lurches to the window and desires to sing.
The panes are timid, huddle up so tight
and in his shadows close together cling.

He staggers darkly round the house-filled streets,
bumps into a child, yells to chase it off,
breathes wheezily at everyone he meets,
mouthing curses in a whispered cough.

In a sodden yard, beside a wall's dark frown,
he romps with rats around a corner space.
A woman in a grey and worn-out gown
makes way for him, the more to hide her face.

A slender thread runs from the fountain yet,
each drop drips down to catch the one that's gone;
he gulps there from a rust-encrusted jet
and helps to wash the ink-black gutters down.

A drunken evening, blue with tipsy light,
lurches to the window, starts to sing and cheer.
The panes all break. Now he, with bloodied sight,
comes bursting in, to wrestle with my fear.

Behind the Wall

I hang like snow from the branches
into the valley's springtime,
like a cold spring I drift in the wind,
I fall damp into the blossoms
as a drop
round which they rot
as if around a bog.
I am the ever-present idea of dying.

I fly, since I cannot walk in peace
through every sky's safe structures,
I upturn pillars and hollow out walls.
Since I cannot sleep at night, I warn
the others with the distant murmur of the sea.
I climb into the mouths of waterfalls,
dislodge clattering scree from the mountains.

I am child of the great world-angst,
which hangs into peace and joy
like the toll of bells into the striding day
and like the scythe into the ripened crop.

I am the ever-present idea of dying.

To the Hoof-beat of the Night

To the hoof-beat of the night, the black stallion at the gate,
my heart still trembles as before and hands me the saddle in flight,
red like the halter lent me by Diomedes.
Strongly the wind gusts before me down the darkened street
and parts the black tresses of the sleeping trees,
so that the fruits, damp from moonlight,
leap scared onto shoulder and sword,
and I fling
the whip onto a dead star.
Only once do I slow my step, to kiss your faithless lips,
already your hair gets caught in the reins,
and your shoe drags in the dust.

And I still hear your breath
and the word with which you struck me.

Spoken to Evening

My doubts, bitter and unsilenced,
seep into the evening's depths.
Weariness sings at my ear.
I listen . . .
That was yesterday already!
That comes and goes again!

I know the sleep-paths to the sweetest pastures.
I'll never walk there again.
I still do not know where the dark lake
concludes the torment.
A mirror is said to lie there,
bright and sealed,
and wants to show us,
gleaming with pain,
the deepest parts.

Without People

Enchanted cloud-mansion, in which we drift . . .
who knows if in this way we do not pass
through many heavens, with eyes glazed ?
We, banished into time
and cast out of space,
we flyers through the night, nowhere to land.

Who knows if we have not already flown round God,
and, since we sped like arrows without seeing him
and hurled our seed still further on
so as to go on living in yet darker generations,
now drift on guiltily?

Who knows if we have not long since been dying?
The cloud-ball around us strives ever higher.
The thin air today already cripples our hands,
and what if the voice should break, our breathing stop . . .?
Does the enchantment stay for the last moments?

The Harbors Were Opened

The harbors were opened. And so we embarked,
the sails were set, with the dream overboard,
steel on our knees and laughter round our hair,
for our oars struck into the sea, swifter than God.

Our oars beat God's shovels and divided the waters;
ahead was the day, and behind stayed the nights,
above was our star and the others were waning below,
outside the storm subsided, and inside our fist swelled up.

Only when a rain-shower flared up did we listen again;
spears hurtled down and angels stepped forward,
clamped on our dark eyes theirs that were darker.
We stood there demolished. Our standard unfurled:

a cross in blood and a larger ship over the heart.

Still I Fear

Still I fear to bind you with the thread of my breath,
to enrobe you in the blue banners of the dream,
to burn torches at the mist-covered gates
of my shadowy mansion, so you may find me . . .

Still I fear to untie you from the shimmering days,
from the gilded descent of the sunlit river of time,
while over the moon's frightening countenance
my heart is seething like silver.

Glance up but do not look at me!
The banners are drooping, the torches are dimmed,
and the moon is describing its beat.
It's time to come and to hold me, sacred deceit!

From

Time on Loan

Outward Voyage

Smoke rises from the land.
Keep the small fisherman's hut in view,
for the sun will go down
before you've covered ten miles.

The dark water, myriad-eyed,
raises the eyelash of foaming white
so as to watch you, large and long,
thirty days long.

Even as the ship stamps firmly
and takes a faltering step,
stand calmly on deck.

At the tables now they
are eating the smoked fish;
then the men will kneel
and patch up the nets,
but at night there comes sleep,
one hour or two hours,
and their hands will be soft,
free of salt and oil,
soft as the bread of the dream
from which they break.

The first wave of the night strikes on the shore,
the second already reaches you.
But if you look sharply across,
you can still see the tree,
defiantly raising its arm –
the wind has already broken off one –
and you think: how much longer,
how much longer will the crooked wood

stand up to the weathering?
There is no more of the land to be seen.
You should have clung with one hand to the sandbank
or pinned yourself by a hair to the cliffs.

Blowing into shells, sea monsters slide
onto the backs of waves, they ride and slash
the days to pieces with gleaming sabers, a red trail
stays in the water, there sleep lays you down
for your remaining hours
and your senses slip away.

Something's happened to the rigging,
you are called for and are glad
that you're needed. The best thing
is working on ships
that travel far,
splicing the ropes, pumping the water,
sealing the bulkheads, and guarding the cargo.
The best thing is to be tired and collapse
in the evening. The best thing in the morning
is to come alive at first light,
to confront the immovable sky,
not to heed the unpassable waters,
and to hoist the ship over the waves
towards that ever returning sun-shore.

Farewell to England

I've hardly set foot on your soil,
silent land, hardly touched a stone;
I was raised up so high by your sky,
so far into clouds, haze, and more distant zones,
that I left you
as I anchored.

You have closed my eyes
with oak leaf and sea breath;
watered by my tears,
you kept your grasses fed;
untied from my dreams,
suns dared to come close;
yet all was gone again
once your day began.
Everything stayed unsaid.

The great grey birds flapped down the streets
and drove me out.
Was I ever here?

I did not want to be seen.

My eyes open wide.
Oak leaf and sea breath?
Among the snakes of the sea
I see, in your stead,
the land of my soul subside.

I have never set foot on its soil.

Fall Down, Heart

Fall down, heart, from the tree of time,
fall, you leaves, from the branches grown cold,
those which the sun once embraced,
fall as teardrops fall from the wide-opened eye.

The curl still waves all day in the wind
around the land-god's suntanned brow,
under the shirt the fist
now presses the gaping wound.

Therefore be hard when the tender back of the clouds
bows to you yet once more,
count it as nothing when Mount Hymettos again
fills your honeycombs.

For a stalk in the drought means little to the farmer,
one summer means little to our great ancestry.

And to what does your heart bear witness?
It swings between yesterday and tomorrow,
soundless and strange,
and what it beats
is already its fall out of time.

Speaking of Darkness

Like Orpheus I play
death on the strings of life,
and to the beauty of the earth
and your eye, which governs heaven,
I speak only of darkness.

Do not forget that you too,
on that morning when your bed
was still damp from the dew
and the carnation slept by your heart,
suddenly saw the dark river
flowing past you.

The string of silence
stretched across the surge of blood,
I plucked the notes of your heart.
Your locks were transformed
into the shadow-hair of night,
and darkness with black flakes
snowed on your countenance.

And I do not belong to you.
So now we both lament.

But, like Orpheus, I know
life on the side of death,
and your eye, closed for ever,
for me is blue.

Paris

Woven to the wheel of night
the lost ones are sleeping
in the thunderous alleys below,
yet where we are is light.

Our arms are full of blossoms,
mimosa from so many years;
gold dust falls from bridge after bridge
breathless to the river.

Cold is the light,
still colder the stone at the gate,
and the bowls of the fountains
are already half emptied.

What will be if we, homesick,
even to our fly-away hair,
stay here and ask: what will be,
if we can cope with the beauty?

Lifted onto the carriage of light,
watchful, what's more, we are lost
in the paths of the spirits above,
yet where we are not is night.

Autumn Maneuvers

I'm not saying that was yesterday. With worthless
summer cash in our pockets we lie again
on the chaff of scorn, on the autumn maneuvers of time.
The escape road to the South is no help to us,
as it is to the birds. Past us, in the evening,
glide fishing smacks and gondolas, and sometimes
a splinter of dream-coated marble strikes me
where I'm vulnerable to beauty, in the eye.

In the papers I read much about the cold
and its consequences, about the foolish and the dead,
about refugees, murderers, and myriads
of ice-floes, yet there's little to my liking.
But then, why is this so? I shut the door
on the beggar who calls at midday, for there is peace
and one can spare oneself the sight, but not
in the rain, the joyless dying of the leaves.

Let us go on a journey. Let us under cypresses
or even under palms or in orange groves
at bargain prices look at sunsets
that have no equals! Let us
forget the unanswered letters to yesterday!
Time works wonders. If it comes uncalled for,
when guilt comes knocking, we are not at home.
In the basement of my heart, sleepless, I find myself again
on the chaff of scorn, on the autumn maneuvers of time.

Time on Loan

Harder days are coming.
The time on loan, repayment due,
appears on the skyline.
Soon you must lace up your boot
and chase the hounds back to the marsh farms.
For the guts of the fish
have turned cold in the wind.
The light of the lupins burns dim.
Your gaze tracks through the murk:
the time on loan, repayment due,
appears on the skyline.

Out there your lover's engulfed in sand,
it climbs round her billowing hair,
it cuts short her words,
it tells her to be silent,
it finds her mortal
and ready to part
after every embrace.

Don't look round.
Lace up your boot.
Chase back the hounds.
Throw the fish in the sea.
Snuff out the lupins!

Harder days are coming.

Stars in March

Sowing is a long way off. On stage come
fledgling fields in the rain and stars in March.
The universe yields to a barren way
of thought, prompted by the light,
which leaves the snow untouched.

Under the snow there will also be dust
and, what didn't rot, the dust's
later foodstuff. Oh breeze that stirs!
The darkness is again ploughed up.
The days are drawing out.

On long days we are sown unasked
in those straight and crooked lines,
and stars go offstage. In the fields
we flourish or decay without choice,
yielding to the rain and finally to the light.

In the Twilight

Again we both put our hands in the fire, you
for the wine of the night that's long been laid down,
I for the morning spring, unknown to the winepress.
We await the bellows of the master, put our trust in him.

Warmed by his task, the glass-blower joins us.
He goes before dawn, he comes before your call,
he is old like the twilight on our withering brows.

Once more he boils the lead in a cauldron of tears,
a glass for you – you'll need it to celebrate your loss –
a smoke-filled pot for me – emptied over the fire.
So I join you and make the shadows ring.

He who now holds back is marked,
he who forgot the keyword is marked.
You cannot and you do not wish to know it,
you drink from the rim, where it is cool
and, as in the past, you drink and stay sober,
your brows are still growing, you still get some looks!

Yet already I, with love, am waiting
for the moment when the pot drops
into the fire, becomes the lead
that once it was. And behind the bullet
I stand, one-eyed, sure of aim and slim,
and fire it off to meet the morning.

Timber and Wood Chips

I'll keep quiet about the hornets,
for they are easily spotted.
Ongoing revolutions
also pose no danger.
Death in the cavalcade of noise
is determined from the start.

But watch out for mayflies
and women, for Sunday huntsmen,
beauticians, the undecided, the well-meaning,
untroubled by any contempt.

From the woods we bore brushwood and logs,
and the sun was slow to rise for us.
Drunk on paper from the conveyor belt,
I no longer make out the branches,
nor the moss, fermented in darker inks,
nor the word carved in the bark,
brazen and true.

Tattered pages, banners,
black posters . . . By day and night,
under these stars and those too,
the faith machine throbs. But on wood,
as long as it's still green, and with gall,
as long as it's still bitter, I willingly
write about how it was at the start.

Be sure you keep awake!
The track of flying wood chips is followed
by the hornets' swarm, and at the fountain
the temptation that once weakened us
makes our hair
stand on end.

Early Noon

The lime tree quietly greens at the start of summer;
far removed from cities, the day-moon
shimmers, palely gleaming. Already it is noon,
already the jet stirs in the fountain,
the crumpled wing of the fairy-tale bird
already pokes out from the rubble,
and the hand deformed by stone-throwing
sinks into the waking corn.

Where Germany's sky blackens the earth,
its beheaded angel seeks a grave for hatred
and hands you the salver of the heart.

A handful of pain recedes across the hill.

Seven years later
it all comes back to you
at the fountain by the gate;
don't gaze in too deeply,
your eyes will flood with tears.

Seven years later
inside a morgue
the hangmen of yesterday
drain the golden goblet.
Your eyes could drown.

Already it is noon, iron writhes
in the ashes, the flag is run up
the pole, and on the rocks
of age-old dream the forged eagle
will henceforth remain.

Only hope cowers, blinded by light.

Release her bonds, lead her down
from the mound, lay your hand
on her eye so that
no shadow may scorch her.
Where Germany's earth blackens the sky,
the cloud searches for words and fills the crater with silence
before summer hears it in a squall of rain.

The unspeakable, quietly spoken, crosses the land;
already it is noon.

Every Day

War is no longer declared
but prolonged. The outrageous
has become the norm. The hero
stays far from the fighting. The weakling
has moved into the firing line.
The day's uniform is patience,
its medal the wretched star
of hope above the heart.

It is awarded
when nothing more happens,
when the bombardment dies down,
when the enemy is no longer seen
and the shadow of eternal weaponry
darkens the sky.

It is awarded
for deserting the flag
for valour when facing the friend,
for betraying despicable secrets,
and for disobeying
every order.

Ingeborg Bachmann

Message

From the corpse-warmed portico of heaven steps the sun.
The immortals are not there,
the fallen are, so we hear.

And splendor will not turn to decay. Our godhead,
history, has ordered us a grave,
from which there is no resurrection.

Night Flight

Our soil is the sky,
tilled in the engines' sweat,
in the face of night,
with the onset of the dream –

dreamt on skull heaps and burning pyres,
under the roof of the world, its tiles
stripped by the wind – and now rain, rain, rain
inside our house and in the mills
the blind flights of the bats.
Who lived there? Whose hands were clean?
Who shone in the night,
a specter to other specters?

Shielded in steel feathers, instruments
cross-examine space, dials and gauges
the shrubbery of the clouds, and love strokes
the forgotten language of our heart:
short and long long . . . For an hour
hail shakes the drum of the ear,
which, ignoring us, listens and goes on.

Sun and earth have not gone down
but just moved like stars, not recognized.

We took off from an airport
where returning doesn't count,
and neither do luggage and loot.
India's spices and silks from Japan
belong to the traders
as fish do to nets.

Yet an aroma may be sensed,

the forerunner of comets,
and the fabric of the air,
rent by comets that have fallen.
Call it the status of the lonely,
in which astonishment occurs.
Nothing else.
We took off, and the cloisters are empty,
since we endure, an order that neither teaches nor heals.
Initiative is not the job of the pilots. Their eyes
are on way points, and spread out on their knees
is the map of the world, to which nothing may be added.

Who lives down there? Who weeps . . . ?
Who loses the key to his house?
Who can't find his bed, who sleeps
in doorways? Who, when morning comes,
dares to explain the silver streak: look, above me . . .
When the water again thrusts into the mill wheel,
who dares to recollect the night?

Psalm

1
Be silent with me, as all the bells are silent

In the afterbirth of horrors
the vermin seek fresh nourishment.
Displayed on Good Friday, a hand
hangs in the sky, two fingers missing,
it cannot swear that all, all this
never was and that nothing
will be. It dips into red clouds,
removes the latest killers,
and goes free.

At night on the earth,
reach through the windows, pull back the sheets
so that the privacy of the sick is laid bare,
an ulcer full of nourishment, endless pain
for every taste.

With gloved hands the butchers check
the breath of those stripped bare,
the moon in the doorway drops to earth,
let the fragments lie, the handle . . .

All was ready for the last rites.
(The sacrament cannot be performed.)

2
How futile all this is.
Heave a city into life,
rise up from this city's dust,
take up a high office,
and dissemble

to escape unmasking.

Keep your promises
before a blind mirror in the air,
before a door locked in the wind.

Untrodden are the paths on the rock-wall of the sky.

3
Oh eyes, seared by the earth, store-house of the sun,
burdened with the rain-load of every eye
and now spun, woven
by the tragic spiders
of the present . . .

4
Into the trough of my silence
place a word
and grow great forests on both sides
so that my mouth
lies all in shadow.

In the Deluge of Roses

Wherever we turn in the deluge of roses,
the night is floodlit by thorns, and the thunder
of leaves, which were so quiet in the bushes,
follows hard on our heels.

From

Invocation of the Great Bear

The Game is Up

Dearest brother, when shall we build a raft
and float across the sky and down?
Dearest brother, our overloaded craft
will founder soon and we shall drown.

Dearest brother, let's draw on paper fair
lots of lands and railway lines.
On those black lines look out, take care,
or you'll be blown up by the mines.

Dearest brother, I'm ready to be tied
screaming and yelling to the stake.
But you from death's dark vale already ride;
together our escape we'll make.

Alert in gypsy camp and desert tent,
we feel the sand run through our hair.
Your age and mine and the world's ages spent
can never be computed year by year.

Don't be fooled by the spider's sticky hand,
by sly ravens, by the feather in the bush.
Neither eat nor drink in Never Never Land,
illusion foams in every pan and dish.

He alone has won who on the bridge of gold
still knows the garnet fairy's code.
I must tell you that all this, like snows of old,
has melted, from the garden flowed.

From many, many stones our feet are sore.
One's sound. Let's skip then till the children's king,

the kingdom's key held gleaming in his jaw,
arrives to fetch us. Then we'll sing:

"Good times are coming when the date stone sprouts!
Each one that falls is on the wing.
Red foxglove makes the hem for paupers' shrouds,
your leaf bud rests on my signet ring."

The game is up. To sleep now, dearest dear.
We go on tiptoe. White nightshirts billow fair.
The house will be bewitched, our parents fear,
if we our breaths should share.

From *About a Land, Its River and Its Lakes*

We settled in a land of flowing springs.
We found the records, showing this whole land,
So boundless and so loved, was ours alone
And could be clasped within your shell-shaped hand.

Who knows when frontiers of the land were fixed
And barbed wire scarified the pine tree's bole?
The mountain stream has swept away the fuse,
The fox expelled the cordite from its hole.

Who knows what people sought on ridge and peak?
A word? We'd stored it safely to be shared.
When said in both our tongues, it sounds more bright,
And when we're silent it will still be paired.

Elsewhere, on passes, barriers are dropped;
Here greetings flow, a bond with bread is sealed.
Each brings his pinch of sky and pouch of earth,
And so the frontier's injuries are healed.

And even though in Babel chaos reigned,
Your tongue became extended, mine got bent –
Those aspirate and labial tones that fool us
Were of that voice that through Judea went.

Since names pervade the interplay of thought,
We talk in symbols and discern their signs.
The snow is not the white that blankets us,
The snow is stillness that within us shines.

To stay unparted we must know what parts us;
In self-same air we feel the self-same slight.

For only green and breeze-filled frontiers heal
With every whisper of the winds of night.

But still we'll want to speak across the frontiers
And frontiers still will run through every word.
Yet, longing to be home, we'll soon come through
And live with every region in accord.

Invocation of the Great Bear

Great Bear, come down, rough-haired night,
cloud-furred with your ancient eyes,
starry eyes.
Through the thicket your padded feet
burst gleaming with their claws,
star claws.
Sharp-eyed we watch our flocks,
though spellbound by you, and we mistrust
your tired flanks and those sharp,
half-uncovered fangs,
old bear.

A fir cone, your world;
you people, its scales.
I drive them, roll them
from the fir trees at the start
to the fir trees at the end.
I nuzzle them, test them in my maw,
and grab at them with my paws.

Be fearful then, or else fear not!
Put money in the poor box and give
the blind man a kind word
so he keeps the bear on its leash.
And season the lambs well.

It could be that this bear
will break loose, no longer threaten,
and hunt down all the fir cones
fallen from the trees, the tall winged ones
that plummeted from paradise.

My Bird

Come what may: the devastated world
sinks back into the twilight,
the woodlands keep a nightcap ready for it,
and from the tower, which the watchman left,
the owl looks down with calm and steady gaze.

Come what may: you know your time,
my bird, you take your veil
and fly through the mist to me.

We peer through the ring of haze where the vermin live.
A nod from me and you swoop out
in a whirl of plumage and down –

My ice-grey shoulder-mate, my weapon,
trimmed with that feather, my only weapon!
My only ornament: that veil and feather of yours.

Even if in the needle-dance below the tree
my skin is burning
and the waist-high thicket
entices me with fragrant leaves,
if my hair-strands quiver,
sway and crave for moisture,
the debris from the stars
drops right onto my hair.

If, helmeted in smoke, I know
once more what's coming,
my bird, my stalwart of the night,
if in the night I am inflamed,
the darkened coppice crackles
and I beat the spark out of me.

If I stay as I am, inflamed
and loved by the fire,
till resin seeps from the tree-trunks,
drips onto the wounds and warmly
spins the earth,
(and even if you rob my heart by night,
my bird so faithful and my bird so true!)
the light shifts to that eerie,
to which, contented
and in majestic calm, you fly –
come what may.

Land Settlement

I came to the grasslands
when it was already night,
scenting out scars in the meadows
and the wind before it stirred.
Love no longer grazed,
the church bells had faded,
and the grass tufts were frayed.

A horn stuck into the ground,
jammed in by the lead beast,
rammed into the dark.

I pulled it from the earth,
I raised it to the sky
with all my strength.

To fill this land
utterly with sound,
I blew on the horn,
determined to live in the coming wind
and among the waving stalks
of whatever origin!

Curriculum Vitae

Long is the night,
long for the man
who cannot die, long
under the streetlamps his raw eye
wavers as does his eye
blinded by schnapps, and the smell
of damp flesh under his nails
does not always numb him, O God,
long is the night.

My hair is not turning white,
for I crept from the womb of machines,
rose-red daubed tar on my forehead
and my locks, they had throttled
her snow-white sister. But I,
the chieftain, strode through the city
of ten times one hundred thousand souls, and my foot
crushed soul-lice under the leather sky,
from which
ten times one hundred thousand pipes of peace
hung coldly. My frequent wish
was the peace of angels
and hunting grounds filled
with the impotent shouting
of my friends.

With legs and arms outspread,
youth climbed like rushes
over me, over muck, over jasmine,
my path led to fabulous nights with the square-
root's mystery, the saga of death
breathes hourly on my window.

Give me milkweed and pour
into my jaws the guffaws
of those grown old before me when I fall
asleep over the folios,
into the shameful dream
that I am no good at thinking
and play with tassels
fringed with snakes.

Our mothers also dreamt
of the future of their menfolk,
saw them as powerful,
revolutionary and lonely,
yet in the garden after prayers,
bending low across the blazing weeds,
hand in hand with the chattering
child of their love. My pathetic father,
why did you all stay silent
and have no second thoughts?

Lost in the fire-fountains,
in a night next to a cannon
that does not fire, damned long
is the night, under the gob-spit
of the jaundiced moon with its bilious
light, a history-trimmed sledge
sweeps over me and away
in the wake of a power dream
(I'm unable to stop it).
I was not asleep; I was awake,
I picked my way between ice-skeletons,
came home, and wound ivy
round arm and leg, white-washed
the ruins with left-over sun.
I kept the holy days,

and only when it was blessed
did I break my bread.

In a grandiose age
one must rush from one light
to another, from one land
to another, under the rainbow,
the compass point in the heart,
the night taken as its radius.
Wide open. From the mountains
lakes are seen, and in the lakes
mountains, and in the cloud-pews
see-saw the bells
of the one world. Whose world
I am forbidden to know.

It happened on a Friday –
I was fasting for my life,
the sky dripped with the juice of lemons
and the bone stuck in my palate –
from the opened-up fish I pulled
a ring, which, cast aside
at my birth, fell into
the river of night and sank.
I tossed it back to the night.

Oh, had I not this fear of death!
Had I the word
(I wouldn't misplace it),
had I not thistles in my heart
(I would rebuff the sun),
had I not greed in my mouth
(I would not drink the white water),
had I not raised an eye-lash
(I would not have seen the cord).

Are they dragging away the sky?
If the earth did not carry me,
I'd long since be lying still,
I'd long since be lying
where the night wants me
before it snorts
and lifts its hoof
for fresh blows,
always a blow.
Always the night.
And no day.

Fog Land

My loved one in winter
is among the beasts of the forest.
The vixen laughs and she knows
I must be back before morning.
How the clouds tremble!
A film of splintering ice
forms on my snow-collar.

My loved one in winter
is a tree among trees and she tempts
the luck-forsaken crows
into her lovely branches. She knows
that the wind in the twilight
lifts her stiffened, frost-trimmed
evening gown and chases me home.

My loved one in winter
is among the fishes and silent.
Drawn to the waters, which the beat
of their fins disturbs from within,
I stand on the bank and watch,
till ice-floes drive me off,
as she dives and she turns.

Startled again by the hunting call
of the bird tensing wide
its wings above me, I fall flat
in the open field; she plucks
the chickens and throws me down
a white collar-bone. I put it round my neck
and walk on through the bitter fluff.

My loved one's unfaithful;

I know she sometimes floats
on her high-heels into town;
in the bars she kisses the glasses
full in the mouth with her straw,
and she has a word for everyone.
But I do not understand this language.

Fog land I have seen,
fog heart I have eaten.

Ingeborg Bachmann

Explain to Me, Love

Your hat is raised in greeting, floats in the breeze,
your uncovered head has tantalized the clouds,
your heart is otherwise engaged,
your mouth takes to itself new languages,
the quaking grass takes over through the land,
while summer blows the asters here and there,
you raise your face, struck blind by cornflowers,

you laugh and weep and are your own undoing,
what will become of you –

Explain to me, love!

In solemn wonder the peacock shows his wheel,
the dove turns up his feathered collar ruff,
the air, too full of cooing, stretches out,
the mallard squawks, the whole land treats itself
to wild honey, even in the tidy park
each bed is circled with a golden dust.

The fish turns pink, it overtakes the shoal
and dives through grottoes into the coral-bed.
The scorpion shyly dances to tunes of silver sands.
The beetle smells from far the finest one;
had I its sense, then I would also feel
that wings shimmer beneath her armored shell
and make my way to the far strawberry bush!

Explain to me, love!

Water knows how to speak,
the whitecap takes the whitecap by the hand,
the grape swells in the vineyard, jumps and falls.

The snail steps unsuspecting from the house!
One stone knows how to soften up another.

Explain to me, love, what I can't explain:
shall I, for this short, terrifying time,
have dealings just with thoughts and all alone
know nothing loving, do nothing loving?
Must a person think? Is he not missed?

You say: another spirit counts on him . . .
So don't explain. I see the salamander
can go through any fire.
No terror drives him, nothing gives him pain.

Days in White

On these days I rise with the birches
and comb the wheat-hair from my brow
before a mirror of ice.

Mingled with my breath,
the milk forms flakes.
So early, it froths easily.
And where I breathe upon the pane,
traced by a child-like hand, your name
appears again: innocence!
After so long a time.

On days like these it doesn't hurt
that I can forget
and must recall.

I'm in love. I am white-hot
with love and give thanks with Hail Marys.
I learnt them on the flight.

On these days I think of the albatross
with which I soared up
and over here,
into an uncharted land.

On the skyline I can sense
over there, brilliant in decline,
my fabled continent,
which dismissed me
in a shroud.

I live and hear from far its swan-song.

Harlem

From all the clouds the staves are slipped,
the rain through every shaft is sieved,
the rain springs off each fire-escape
and tinkles on the hurdy's tunes.

The black-skinned city rolls its eye-whites
and leaves the world round every bend.
The rain-rhythms are infiltrated by silence.
The rain-blues are switched off.

Dead Harbor

Clammy flags hang there on the masts
in hues no land has ever known,
they wave for mud-bespattered stars
and the moon at rest, green in the crow's-nest.

World of water from the age of discovery!
Waves now overgrow each thoroughfare;
up above the light drips from the mesh
of new roads displaced into the air.

Down there the waters leaf through the bibles,
the compass needle points to night.
Out of the dreams the gold is filtered,
the sea is left to its abandoned plight.

No land, not one, remained untrodden!
The seaman's twine drifts in tatters,
for those wild, guffawing adventurers
fell into the dead arm of the waters.

Say and Hearsay

Don't issue from our mouth,
word that sows the dragon seed.
It's true the air is close,
light seethes, sours, and ferments,
and over the swamp a midge-haze darkly hangs.

The hemlock likes to tipple,
a cat's skin is on show,
the serpent hisses at it,
the scorpion starts his dance.

Don't penetrate our ear,
rumor of others' guilt.
Word, die in the swamp
from which the pool wells up.

Word, be one of us
with tender patience,
impatience too. This sowing
must come to an end.

He who imitates the beast's sound will not outdo the beast.
He who betrays the secret of his bed forfeits any love.
The word's bastard serves the joke to victimize a fool.

Who wants a judgement from you on this stranger?
And if you give it uninvited, walk on from night to night,
his blisters on your feet, walk! Don't come back.

Word, be one of us,
broad-minded, lucid, nice.
Surely there must be an end
to all this inhibition.

(The crab draws back,
the mole sleeps too long,
the soft water loosens
the chalk that spun the stones.)

Come, grace of breath and sound,
strengthen this mouth
when its frailty
horrifies and holds us back.

Come and don't give up,
since we are in dispute with so much evil.
Before dragon blood protects the foe,
I'll put this hand into the fire.
Rescue me, my word.

The First-Born Land

To my first-born land, to the South,
I came and found, waist-deep in the sea,
impoverished and bare,
town and citadel.

Trampled by dust into sleep,
I lay in the light;
a skeletal tree hung over me,
leafed in Ionian salt.

There no dream fell down from it.

There no rosemary blooms,
no bird refreshes
its song in springs.

In my first-born land, in the South,
the viper struck at me
and the horror in the light.

O close,
close your eyes!
Press your mouth to the bite!

And as I drank myself
and earth-tremors rocked
my first-born land,
I woke up clear-sighted.

Life was granted me there.

There the stone is not dead.
The wick flares up
when lit by a glance.

Songs from an Island

Shadow fruits are falling from the walls,
moonlight bathes the house, and ash
from dead volcanoes is borne here on the ocean wind.

Embraced by handsome youths,
the coasts are sleeping,
your flesh remembers mine,
it had a liking for me
already when the ships
cast off from land and crosses
bearing our mortal load
did duty for our masts.

The gallows now stand empty,
they seek and find us gone.

―――――――――

When you rise from the dead,
when I rise from the dead,
no stone is at the gate,
no boat rests on the sea.

Tomorrow barrels will roll
towards the Sunday waves,
we come on anointed
feet to the beach, to wash
the grapes and tread
the harvest into wine,
tomorrow on the beach.

When you rise up again,
when I rise up again,

the hangman dangles at the gate,
the hammer sinks into the sea.

Sometime the feast must come!
Saint Anthony, you who have suffered,
Saint Leonard, you who have suffered,
Saint Vitus, you who have suffered.

Room for our pleas, for those who pray,
room for music and for joy!
We have learnt restraint,
we sing in the choir of cicadas,
we eat and we drink,
the scrawny cats
slink around our table
till evening mass begins,
I hold you by the hand
with my eyes,
and to you a calm, brave heart
offers up its desires.

Honey and nuts for the children,
bulging nets for the fishermen,
fruitfulness for the gardens,
moon for the volcano, moon for the volcano!

Our sparks leapt across borders,
Across the night rockets
cartwheeled their way, on darkened floats
the cavalcade moves on, makes room
for a primeval time
of slithering lizards,
of feasting plants,
of frenzied fish,
of the wind's orgies and the mountain's

joy, when a pious star
goes astray, slams into its chest
and scatters into dust.

Now be steadfast, foolish saints,
tell the mainland that the craters do not rest!
Saint Roch, you who have suffered,
O you who have suffered, Saint Francis.

Anyone who leaves must throw his hat,
filled with mussels that were gathered
through the summer, into the sea
and travel with billowing hair,
he must plunge the table that he laid
for his lover into the sea,
he must empty the dregs of wine
left in his glass into the sea,
he must give his bread to the fish
and mix into the sea a drop of blood,
he must thrust his knife deep into the waves,
and sink his shoe,
heart, anchor and cross,
and sail with billowing hair!
Then he will come again.
When?
Don't ask.

There is fire under the earth,
and the fire is pure.

There is fire under the earth
and molten stone.

There is a river under the earth
that runs into us.

There is a river under the earth
that scorches our bones.

A mighty fire will come,
a river will flow over the earth.

We shall be witnesses.

Roman Nightscape

When the see-saw carries off the seven hills
into the sky, it also slides,
embraced by us and weighed down,
into the dark water,

dips us into the river-mud, till in our laps
the fish crowd together.
When our turn comes,
we push off.

The hills sink down,
we rise up and share
every fish with the night.

Neither jumps off.
So certain is it that love alone
uplifts, and each of us the other.

Black Waltz

The oar comes in with the black waltz at the gong,
shadows with blunt jabs stitch in the guitar's song.

Under the sill my darkened house in the mirror glares,
candelabras gently marked by their pointed flares.

Stretched over the sounds: contract of wave and game,
the sea-bed slips away with a different aim.

The market cries and the blue balloon I owe to the day –
stone-rump and bird-swoop make their own way

to their nightly pas de deux, they silently swing,
O Venice, Eastern and Western land, on piles, on the wing!

Only mosaics take root, maintaining their poise,
the pillars danced round by frescoes, grotesques, and buoys.

August was never created for seeing the lion-sun,
it shook out its mane when summer'd begun.

The slap of paws on the bow, think pagan dazzle,
the mad masquerade in the wake of the vessel.

Swamped paving, a banner is hoisted above,
brackish water, then love and the odour of love.

Intro, then the upbeat for silence, no further key,
oars beating pauses and a coda from the sea.

Ingeborg Bachmann

Shadow Roses Shadow

Under a foreign sky
shadow roses
shadow
on a foreign soil
between roses and shadow
in a foreign water
my shadow

Agrigento

Bearing limpid water in its hands,
at noon of the day with its whitened crown
the river will observe itself deep down
and one last time will redirect the sands,
carrying limpid water in its hands.

If the wind from eucalyptus groves
bears sharply-colored, feathery leaves,
the river will adore the deeper weaves.
The steady patter of the flinty stones
is borne on wind to eucalyptus groves.

Hallowed by light and silent fire-brands,
the sea keeps the ancient shrine on show;
the river, ruffled to where it starts its flow,
carrying limpid water in its hands,
is sanctified by silent fire-brands.

To the Sun

Fairer than the acclaimed moon and its ennobled light,
Fairer than the stars, the famous orders of the night,
Much fairer than the fiery passage of a comet,
And called to much greater beauty than any other star,
Since my life and yours daily depend on it, here is the sun!

Fair sun which, rising, has been mindful of its task
And finished it, most lovely in the summer, when on the coasts
A day turns to vapor and, softly mirrored, the sails
Pass before your eyes until you tire and the last is cut short.

Without the sun art must take the veil again,
You appear no more to me, and the sea and the sand,
Lashed by shadows, flee beneath my gaze.

Fair light that keeps us warm, preserves us with marvelous care,
So I see again, and so I see you again!

Nothing more fair under the sun than to be under the sun . . .

Nothing more fair than to see a floating twig and the bird above,
Reflecting on its flight, and down below a shoal of fish,
Colored, shaped, and sent into the world on a mission of light,
And to see around me the quadrant of a field, the jagged outline of my land
And the dress you have put on. And the dress, bell-shaped and blue!

Fair blue, in which peacocks strut and take their bow,

Blue of distances, zones of joy with weather for my mood,
The sky-line blue by chance! And my delighted eyes
Open wide again and sparkle until they burn sore.

Fair sun, to whom even from dust the greatest praise is due,
Therefore, and not because of moon and stars, and not
Because the night boasts of its comets and tries to make a
fool of me,
But for your sake and soon endlessly and for that alone
I shall lament the certain fading of my eyes.

Songs of Escape

Durra legge d'Amor! Ma, ben che obliqua,
Servar convensi; pero ch'ella aggiunge
Di cielo in terra, universale, antiqua.
                    Petrarca, 'I Trionfi'

I
In snow the palm twig snaps,
the stairways crash below,
the town lies rigid, gleams
in winter's eerie glow.

The children shriek and move
on up the hunger hill,
they worship God on high,
of white flour eat their fill.

The gaudy frills of winter,
the mandarins' old gold,
are caught in gusting wind,
the blood orange then is rolled.

II
But here I lie alone,
enmeshed in wounded ice.

The snow has not as yet
blindfolded my two eyes.

The dead, pressed close against me,
are quiet in every tongue.

No one loves me, no lamp
has yet for me been swung.

III
The isles, the Sporades,
fair patchwork in the sea,
watered by icy streams,
still bend their fruits to me.

The white rescuers, the ships –
oh lonely sailor's hand! –
they point, before they sink,
way back toward the land.

IV
Cold like none before has broken through.
Airborne forces came across the sea.
The Gulf with all its lights has given in,
The city has fallen.

I am innocent and captive
in subjugated Naples, where the winter
sets Posillipo, Vomero in the sky,
where with white flashes it cleans things up
among the songs
and it gives the husky thunderclaps
what's theirs by right.

I am innocent, and right to Camaldoli
the pine trees touch the clouds;
and without solace, for the rain
will not soon strip the palms;
without hope, for I shall not escape,
even if the fish tenses its guardian fins
and if the mist on the winter beach,
thrown up by waves for ever warm,
builds a wall for me,
even if the waves
fleeing

deprive those fleeing
of their nearest goal.

V
Away with snow from the spice-filled town!
The breath of fruits must pass through the streets.
Scatter the currants,
bring on the figs, the capers!
Give new life to the summer,
new life to the cycle,
birth, blood, vomit, and phlegm,
death – claw into the scars,
imprint the lines
on faces,
distrustful, idle, old,
etched out in chalk and drenched in oil,
sly from bargaining,
familiar with danger,
the rage of the lava god,
the angel smoke
and the damnable glow.

VI
Instructed in love
by ten thousand books,
taught through the handing down
of barely changing gestures
and stupid oaths –

initiated into love
but not till here –
when the lava flowed down
and its breath struck us
at the mountain's foot,
when at last the exhausted crater

yielded up the key
to these imprisoned bodies.

We stepped into enchanted rooms,
lighting up the darkness
with our fingertips.

VII
In there your eyes are windows
into a land in which I stand revealed.

In there your breast is a sea
that draws me to to its bed.
In there your hip's a landing-stage
for my ships, those sailing back
from too distant voyages.

Fortune weaves a silver rope
by which I lie tethered.

In there your mouth is a downy nest
for my fledgling tongue.
In there your flesh is melon-light,
sweet and enjoyable without end.
In there your veins are restful
and quite filled with the gold
which I wash with my tears
and which will one day make up for me.

You receive awards, your arms hug worldly goods,
which are granted first to you.

In there your feet are never on the move
but have already reached my velvet lands.
In there your bones are shining flutes,

from which I can conjure up sounds
that also will enrapture death . . .

VIII
. . . Earth, sea and sky.
Crumpled by kisses,
the earth,
the sea and the sky,
the earth
enfolded still by my words,
the sea and the sky
enfolded still by my last word!

Afflicted by my sounds,
this earth which, sobbing in my teeth,
dropped anchor
with all its blast furnaces, towers
and arrogant peaks,

this beaten earth
which laid bare before me its ravines,
its steppes, deserts, and tundras,

this restless earth
with its twitching magnetic fields,
which bound itself here
with chains of force yet unknown to it,

this numbed and numbing earth
with deadly nightshade,
leaden poisons
and streams of fragrance —

descended in the sea,
ascended in the sky,
the earth!

IX
The black cat,
the oil on the ground,
the evil eye:

Disaster!

Take down the coral horn,
hang the horns outside the house,
darkness, no light!

X
O love, which cracked open
and cast out our shells, our shield,
weatherguard and brown rust of the years!

O sorrows, which stamped out our love,
its dampened fire in our feeling parts!
Smoke-filled, dying in smoke, the flame goes into itself.

XI
You want the summer lightning, you throw the knives,
you strip the warm veins out of the air;

dazzling you, out of the open pulses
the last of the fireworks soundlessly leap:

madness, contempt, and then revenge,
remorse already, then denial.

You're still aware your blades are blunted,
and finally you feel how love concludes:

with honest thunderstorms and with pure breath
it claps you into the dungeon of dreams.

Where its golden hair hangs flowing down,
you snatch at it, the ladder to the void.

The rungs are a thousand and one nights high.
The step into the vacuum is the last.

And where you land, there the old places are,
to every place you give three drops of blood.

Demented, you hold onto rootless curls.
The bell rings out, and that must be enough.

XII
Mouth which has passed the night in my mouth,
eye that has watched over my eye,
hand –

and the eyes that challenged me,
mouth which passed the sentence,
hand which put me to death!

XIII
The sun does not warm, voiceless is the sea.
No one takes apart the snow-packed graves.
Is no brazier being filled
with glowing ash? Yet ash won't do.

Redeem me! I cannot go on dying.

The saint has other things to do;
he frets about the city and goes for bread.
The washing line hardly holds up the sheet,
Which soon will fall. Yet it won't cover me.

I am still guilty. Lift me up.
I am not guilty. Lift me up.

Prise the ice-grain from the frozen eye,
Burst in with a stare,
search for the blue depths,
swim, look and dive.

It's not me.
It is me.

XIV
Wait for my death and then hear me again,
the snow-basket tips, and the water sings,
all sounds merge into the Toledo, it's thawing,
a melody melts the ice.
O mighty thaw!

Set your sights high!

Syllables in the oleander,
word in the acacia's green,
cascades from the wall.

Music,
bright and rippled,
fills the fountains.

XV
Love has one triumph and death has one,
time and the time thereafter.
We have none.

Only setting of stars around us. Silence and afterglow.
But the song above the dust
then will rise above us.

From

Poems 1957-1961

Hôtel de la Paix

The rose-load falls silent from the walls,
and through the carpet shine earth and soil.
The heart-light of the lamp fades.
Darkness. Steps.
The bolt has slid across in front of death.

Exile

I am a dead man who roams
unknown in the Prefect's realm
and has no fixed abode
surplus in the golden cities
and in the greening land

long since dispensed with
furnished with nothing

Only with wind with time and with sound

I who cannot live among people

I with the German language
as this cloud around me
which I keep as a house
and urge through all the tongues

Oh how the cloud darkens
the dark tones those of rain
only a few of them fall

Then it bears the dead man up into brighter zones

Miriam

Where did you obtain your raven hair,
your charming forename with the almond cast?
It's not from youth you gleam with morning light,
your land's been morning a millennium past.

Promise us Jericho, wake up the psalter,
yield up the source of Jordan from your hand
and turn to stone the killers so surprised
and, for a moment too, your second land.

Touch every breast of stone and work the wonder
that even the tear will overrun the stone.
And be baptized with the warm water. Stay
unknown to us, till to ourselves we're more unknown.

Snow will often fall into your cradle.
Beneath the blades the scrape of ice will start.
By your deep sleep the world is overcome.
The Red Sea draws back, its waters part.

Current

So far in life and now so near to death,
no one to dispute this with at hand,
from out the earth I tear away my part,

Then deep into the calm ocean's heart
plunge the green clod and wash myself to land.

Tin birds rise up and scent of cinnamon!
With my murderer, time, I'm alone.
Blue-drunk, into pupas we've grown.

Safe Conduct

With sleep-drunk birds
and trees shot through with wind
the day gets up, and the sea
empties over it a foaming beaker.

The rivers surge to the open sea,
and the land, rich with fresh flowers,
puts promises of love
into the pure air's mouth.

The earth does not wish to wear a mushroom cloud,
nor to spew up any creature under heaven,
but with rain and anger's lightning flash
to confound the monstrous prophecies of doom.

It wants to see awaken with us
our gaudy brothers and our pallid sisters:
King Fish, Her Highness Nightingale
and that Prince of Fire the Salamander.

For us it plants corals in the sea,
commands forests to be silent,
the marble's vein to swell,
the dew once more to pass across the ashes.

Each day from out of night the earth
desires safe conduct to the cosmos
that for a thousand and one mornings there shall be
the youthful blessings of an ancient beauty.

You Words

For Nelly Sachs, friend and poet, in admiration

You words, up and follow me!
And if we've already moved on,
moved on too far, let's just this once
go further, let's go without an end.

Ahead no brightness.

The word
will just
draw other words after it,
phrase by phrase.
So world might
in the end
impose itself,
be already said.
So do not say it.

Words, follow me,
let none of this be final –
not this word-lust,
not saying and gainsaying!

Let for a while now
none of the feelings speak,
let the heartstrings
work on other things.

Let, I say, let be.

To the highest ear, dear friend,
let, I say, no whisper come,

give not a thought to death.
Let be, and follow me, and be not meek,
not bitter yet,
not comforting,
but comfortless,
insignificant,
and hence not void of signs.

And this least of all: the image
in the cobweb, the empty dirge
of syllables, of dying words.

Not a dying word,
you words!

From

Poems 1964-1967

Truly

For Anna Achmatova

Those whom a word has never thwarted
(and I say this to all of you),
those who simply help themselves,
and with words too –

they cannot be helped,
not in the short term
nor in the long,

to make a single lasting sentence,
to survive in the ding-dong of words.

No one writes this sentence
who does not sign below.

Bohemia Lies on Sea

If houses hereabouts are green, I'll step inside a house.
If bridges here are sound, I'll tread on solid ground.
If love's labor's lost for ever, I'll gladly lose it here.

If it's not me, it's somebody; he's as good as I.

If I'm bordered by a word, then leave me bordered.
If Bohemia's still on sea, then I believe the seas again.
And if I still believe in sea, then I hope for land.

If it's me, it's anybody; he's worth as much as I.
For me, there's nothing more I want. I want to go under.

Under – that means to sea; I find Bohemia there again.
Driven under, I wake up calm.
Up again, I fully understand and am not lost.

Come here, all you Bohemians, seamen, harbor whores, and ships
unanchored. Don't you want to be Bohemian, Illyrians,
Veronesi,
and Venetians all? Act out the comedies that make us laugh

and bring us tears. And stray a hundred times,
as I once strayed and never once stood up to trials,
and yet I have withstood them, time and time again.

As Bohemia withstood them and one fine day
was freed to join the sea and lies by water now.

I'm bordered still by a word and by another land,
I'm bordered, if only a bit, by all things more and more,

a Bohemian, a renegade, having nothing, tied by nothing, able still to spy, from this disputed sea, land that's mine by choice.

Prague, January 64

Since that night
I can walk and talk again.
Things sound Bohemian;
as if I was home again,

where, between the Moldau, the Danube,
and my childhood river,
everything bears my imprint.

Step by step, walking has come back to me;
looked at, I've learnt to see again.

Bent over, blinking,
I hung from the window,
saw the shadow years,
in which no star
hung in my mouth,
move off across the hill.

At six in the morning
snow clearers from the Tatra,
with their great chapped paws,
swept the fragments of this ice-blanket
across the Castle Square.

Under the splintering slabs
of my river – yes, it's mine too –
the freed water streamed out.

It was heard right to the Urals.

A Kind of Loss

Shared in use: seasons, books and a tune.
The keys, the teacups, the bread-basket, sheets and a bed.
A trousseau of words, of gestures, brought with me,
employed, consumed.
House rules adhered to. Spoken. Done. And always the
proffered hand.

I fell in love with winter, with a Viennese septet, with
summer.
With atlases, with a mountain hide-out, with a beach and a
bed.
Practiced a cult with dates, declared promises to be binding,
worshipped a Something and was devout when faced with a
Nothing,

(- the folded newspaper, the cold ash, the scrap of paper
with a note)
fearless in religion, for this bed was the church.

Out of the sea-view came my inexhaustible painting.
From the balcony there were peoples, my neighbors to greet.
By the fire-side, safe from harm, my hair had its brightest
sheen.
The ring at the door was the signal for my joy.

It's not you I've lost,
but the world.

Enigma

For Hans Werner Henze from the time of the ariosi

Nothing more will come.

Spring will no longer happen.
Thousand-year calendars foretell this to all.

But summers too and whatever else has pleasant labels
such as "summery" –
nothing more will come.

You really shouldn't cry,
the music says.

Otherwise
no one
says
a word.

No Frills

Nothing else appeals to me.

Shall I
dress up a metaphor
with an almond blossom?
Crucify the syntax
for a trick of light?
Who will cudgel his brains
over such trifles?

I have gained insight
with the words
that are there
(for the underclass)

hunger
        shame
                tears
and
                        darkness.

I can make do
with uncleansed sobbing,
with despair
(and in desperation I still despair)
at so much misery,
at the sickness figures, at the cost of living.

I do not neglect my writing,
just myself.
Heaven knows,
others know how

to help themselves with words.
I am not my assistant.

Shall I
take a thought prisoner,
take it for grilling to a lighted cell?
Treat both eye and ear
to first-rate word-morsels?
research the libido of a vowel?
Explore the valuation of our consonants?

Must I
with my hail-battered head,
with writer's cramp in this hand,
tear apart the scraps of paper
under pressure from three hundred nights,
sweep away the concocted word-operas,

thus destroying: I thou and he she it
we you?

(So I should. The others should.)

My part, it can get lost.

From

I Know No Better World

My Poems Have Gone Astray

My poems have gone astray.
I search for them in every corner of the room.
Don't know in my pain how to write
a pain, know nothing more at all.

Know that one cannot just keep blathering on,
more spice is needed, a seasoned metaphor
should come to mind. But with the knife in my back.

Parlo e tacio, I escape into an idiom,
in which even some Spanish occurs, los toros y
los planetas, perhaps still to be heard
on some old stolen record. A bit of French
would also do, tu es mon amour depuis si longtemps.

Adieu, you lovely words, with all your promises.
Why have you abandoned me? Were you not well?
I have put you on deposit with a heart, one of stone.
Work for me there, keep at it there, do a job for me there.

I Know No Better World

Let him who knows a better world step forward.
Alone, no longer boldly, and with this spittle not wiped off,
this spittle still worn on his face,
as if for the coronation and, that score settled, on to communion,
among his friends. The feeble guinea-pig,
the rat, and those who perish, all of them,
not alone, what's more, a real terror,
a dream of a comeback,
dreaming of being armed, dreaming
of a comeback.

Till Your Return

Till your return. But they say
you'll never be back. There's just
another night to come.

Still not forgiven,
how true with those wild
accusations in my head,
still not understood
that this creature doesn't have to be respected,
still not realized
what it is to fight someone
who refuses to fight.
I refuse, appeal
to the heart in you that,

in case you lack one, has been
implanted in you by me.

I have implanted in you a heart,
practised at times a cult
of fervor for its gentle throbs.
I have implanted my friendly nature,
my laughter and a music for the future
into the drought of a breast sucked dry.
I've doted, loved like creatures of the wild,
enthused by love and by each day.
Worshipped, burnt roots, made every trifle
a celebration, repeated parrot-fashion
every word and forgot where I belong.
I had not been like this for ages.

But who am I now? I myself,
no longer used to swallowing fire.
My heart no longer beats.
How will this end? I have become

tedious and so sluggish and so cold
that without my pain I would not be alive.

Goodbye

The flesh that has aged so well with me,
the parchment hand that kept mine cool,
let it lie on that whitened thigh,
let flesh grow young again, in an instant,
so that decay takes hold more swiftly.
The lines have come swiftly, everything above
the taut muscle frame already somewhat sunken.

Not to be loved. The pain could be greater.
Lucky the one whose door slams shut.
But the flesh – with the fault line on the knee,
the wrinkled hands, all appearing overnight,
the weathered shoulder blade, where no green grows –
once it was shelter for a face.

Aged by a hundred years in a day.
The trusting beast, under the lash of the whip,
is robbed of pre-established harmony.

Smells

I've always loved the smell, the sweat,
the morning effluvia, and the excrement,
the filth from a long rail-trip and in a bed.

My smell has been damned, I reeked
of liquor in a well-ordered house.
Three baths a day no rarity. By month's end
I have been avoided like a corpse.

I have regretted much, but most of all my smell.
Most of all that my smell has not been liked.
That breeds hatred; vengefulness and damnation too are bred.

The Child

For sure there might have been yet
poorer children., there's always one more
who's worse off still and even quieter.
Crippled child, the time's arrived
to bury you – from eight to eight
every day and even at night
the doors are still open – to bring
this horror to an end,
to put up the sign Closed.
Performing my dramas,
inaccessible, even to me,
stops me going on to others.
So much is alive, is lived.
If I shut the door on you,
it is not because I forget.
But both of us must come to rest,
you've long been saying this to me.
I'm leaving you in peace, as in
a compact which says after turmoil
that could drive you mad: 'Here lie our limits'.
This may go counter to our nature,
our reason's here at hand
to undertake the slight correction,
to put down markers, as in the compact.

Glory Street

The blessing of morphine, but not the blessing of a letter,
the blessing of people, words, talk, but only in delirium,
that sole phenomenon that everyone awaits,
no coming back in a lifetime, only transfiguration.

Evil lasts, errors do not,
the forgivable is long forgiven, the knife wounds
are likewise healed, only the slash that evil makes
does not heal; it flares up at night, every night.

Farewell

We shall be the furthest, no greeting
will be returned any more, no word is still
worth employing. Also the microbe under
the glass, the guinea pig too on which
an experiment ends fatally and which,
twitching and poisoned, can no longer
cry out to the Lord, these are my comrades,
I look for all mistreated creatures,
those worn out and the thrown-away glass,
the discarded garments, the burnt-out houses that shriek
to heaven, and I make do with what's left.
All these are my kindred.
Brotherly love is practiced on us, we are patched up,
instilled with trust and moved
to another place.

This place is good, here we are still
reachable only by death, a stupid guinea pig,
a squashed louse, a blissful heart,
reachable no longer by naked fear,
cloaked in the pauper's smock of brotherly love.

The Line of Life

At night I dream.

Tonight I dream that someone
reading my hand points out the line
is cut off short, forms a crack, and I saw one,
two, three deaths, nothing but
deaths
and in the morning pressed my wet flannel
to the spot, I pulled up the window,
that too reached the spot,
I put the tea on, that too
reached this spot, everything
reached this crack and that
was what I saw while awake.

I want to fall apart like some old dress,
develop rickety joints, shrink
as the apple shrinks, get tiny, ancient and stone-grey
and one day, bent low, lie down
under a root and laugh
at all the deaths and gently fade away,
so that I scarcely notice where I start
to stop, where I stop belonging.

Gently, Softly

Even if it's just starting,
starting, gently, softly,

can't you see it friends,
can't you? For

who would wish to live
if he has no air
to breathe, the black
sail always hoisted.

Who would wish to live
if he has no air to breathe,
the black sail always hoisted.
Day just one night
night just a day,
when all is lost and
does not come back and
never will come back.

By day the waste land
still loved by those hated.

So We Might Die

So we might die,
not to be parted;
your house must
remain my house.
I must go in and out,
must remain there,
see things are right,
since no one else sees
what your withered eyes
find at evening, just me,
I know, hence your house
must always
be my house
wherever I am. I must
see to the evening
and lift the thoughts
up into sleep.

How Difficult Forgiving Is

How difficult forgiving is,
such a slow and gruelling task,
it's been my only occupation
for so many years.

Hatred has made me ill,
I'm disfigured, these puss-filled boils
still won't let me show myself
in company.

I know only that I
cannot go on hating like this,
cannot wish for your death,
which I do not wish for at all
or by my hand.

I have learnt that I
must love my enemies, and
this is so easy, for how then
should my enemies
do me worse than evil?
If a bullet goes astray,
if someone spits in my face,
as yesterday, I have no scruples
about the love prescribed for me.

I am afraid of the love
you have instilled in me
with the cruellest intent.
Quite rotted by searing acids,
by all that arsenic, the opium,
quite numbed by my destruction.
Since I no longer live in you

and am already dead where I am.
Counting the bars, surviving,
feeding myself twice a day,
then going to the toilet,
begging for the means
to plunge me into sleep for a year.

I Lose My Screams

I lose my screams
as someone else loses
his money, his cash,
his heart, I lose
my huge screams
all over Rome,
in Berlin I lose
screams, real ones,
in the streets until
my brain turns blood-red
inside, I lose everything,
except I do not lose
the horror of it that
one can lose screams
every day and
everywhere.

Night of Love

In a night of love after a long night
I have learnt to speak again and I wept
because a word came out of me. I have learnt to walk again,
walked up to the window and said hunger and light
and night was right by me for light.

After an overlong night
slept peacefully again,
trusting in this,

I spoke more easily in the dark,
spoke on through the day,
ran my fingers over my face,
I am no longer dead.
A bush, from which fire struck in the night.
My avenger stepped out and called himself life.
I even said: let me die, and meant
without fear my more welcome death.

Wenceslas Square

Not much to see, ice tracks, snow piles,
mouths steaming from the cold, people
up and down like shoals of fish,
toing and froing – not much to understand –
mingling and jostling with one another,

just steaming, clouding, each keeps his thoughts
to himself, thinks nothing. What for
and why here?

The square from which I make for home is so called,
is one and the same. I have my little puff of steam
before my face and turn off and arrive alive
in a lane that ends deep in my past,
where my origins are.

Jewish Cemetery

Forest of stone, no special graves, nowhere to kneel
and nowhere for flowers. Each stone is so cramped there,
as if clinging to the other's neck, none unmindful of the
other,
offering the living a hair's breadth to pass through
without grief. On reaching the exit, you have not death
but the day in your heart.

Renunciation

My skin still bears a breath,
my hand still holds his manhood,
my mouth still arches over midnight,
my desire is still for you.
What is my desire, if not for you?

Oh how good that no-one knows,
if you wish to make me wretched,
then begin again.

Again and Again, Black and White

Again my mouth arches over midnight.
A swarthy tongue arouses in me a note
with which I hung on you in sobs; all night,
all day I let in light and am not cleansed.
My skin has been pigmented by yours.
How good that no-one knows what you are called,
that my young blackness stems from yours that's old,
from yours that's ancient, indigenous.
You call to me like the Queen of the Zambesi.

Strangers in the Night

In November and on into December,
I have to laugh, that was
a lifetime for me;
the telephone turned pale,
rang in a different way,
the cigarettes scorched
my fingers, and then
the birds scorched the heavens
with their southward calls.
We spoke at a distance
and Jerusalem, my own,
kept coming to mind.

What cruelty
to scratch my skin;
no longer can
my heart be touched.
I talk and laugh and talk.
No longer to be touched.

But the birds with their
terrifying calls.
I have set aside
a feeling and I
had one final one.

How tired I am and how I laugh
and show myself where the birds
have done their writing, and I say nothing,
there's nothing more to say, nothing more.
Only in November and even in December
I wrote your name in the snow
and was overjoyed.

This was the finest time.
It's not for me to give thanks,
the early winter had
a stroke of luck with me, with
both of us, perhaps.
Where are you? That is not a question.
I know full well. I am old
and wise also, the grave is dug,
there's no mistaking it.
Youth, the eternal light,
I have never seen it.
But I make my plea for being young.
I make my plea for you.
A few weeks were given me
of what is youth, and I knew
I have no share in it.
I would like to be young, since I never was,

I am just accepted, following disasters,
and I am tolerated.

Miscellaneous Poems

Libraries

The bookshelves sag,
the volumes burdened with the past.
Their sweat is dust,
their sensation numbness.
They've given up the fight.
They have escaped
to the Island of Knowledge.
Some have lost all conscience.
But here and there people's fingers
stick out of them
and point directly at life
or at the sky.

The Visitor

At times Someone comes
from a strange land,
strangely dressed,
with a strange tongue.
Yet when you look Him in the eye,
you comprehend
that He comprehends.
You lean your head against his shoulder
and begin to speak of things
about which He would never ask:
that the wind strikes right into your heart,
that you feel the stars right into your blood,
that you . . .
He stands, hears and understands.
You can press your whole body against His,
wrap your arms around Him . . .
And so you have Him,
have yourself,
until midnight!

Waiting Room

Language no longer unites.
What we share is waiting.
A chair
a bench
a window
through which light falls
into our room
onto our hands
onto our eyes
and also
onto the floor.
Heal our eyes
so that we again find words,
bright ones that I can say to you.

Jacob's Wheel

Plane trees, encircled by cold, stood there before me,
wind at the gates pulled my dress more tightly about me,
and you called me into the house where you were sent for the
night-time.

This side and that of the Rhine, the windows stayed shuttered;
we opened one up in order to hope in the darkness
over the wheel of your people, those who were buried in
water.

Did I enfold you? You were meant not to notice the bridges,
those blown up to the clouds and ripped into pieces.
Ask: so you cheated both me and the wheel in the face of the
fallen?

Going home along banks in pursuit of new tideways,
I carried the wheel, it spoke for your life in the future;
so from now on let no wind woo the leaves of the plane trees,

let no eye ever break that observes more deeply than others,
and the children of Israel shall be untouched by water.

William Turner: Backlight

Across a land with meagre sun
he stretched his canvas and brushed in
the tracks reaching for the sky.
He knew:
what matters is the fall of light.

To himself he gave little thought
and allowed himself no perspective.

Afterword

I

Ingeborg Bachmann was born between the two world wars in Klagenfurt, Carinthia, on 25 June 1926. She grew up in a teacher's family and had a secure childhood. The Hitler invasion of Austria and its annexation by Nazi Germany left her traumatized: "It was horrendous that my recollection starts from this day, with a premature anguish unequalled by anything I would later experience" (Interview, 24 December 1971, *Conversations and Interviews*, p. 111). In her first full-length story, *The Honditsch Cross* (1943), the seventeen-year-old writer confronted the Nazi state and its ideology of war with her Utopian borders of peoples and languages; she saw war as nothing less than the staging of wholesale murder.

The boundary mentality, both inward and outward, was characteristic of Carinthians even before the advent of the Nazi dictatorship. In Hitler's state it became a murderous reality and posed an initial and lasting challenge for the young author. From then on her answer was the Utopia of frontiers shared and harmonious neighborliness. "But still we'll want to speak across the frontiers / and frontiers still will run through every word. / Yet, longing to be home we'll soon come through / and live with every region in accord," is how she put it in "About a Land, its River and its Lakes," the great biographical poem in her second book of poetry, *Invocation of the Great Bear* (1956). Then in her late poem "Bohemia Lies on Sea," published in 1968, which Bachmann claimed as her favorite, she saw the intermingling of people across the frontier divide as the Utopian salvation of the writer's task: "I'm bordered still by a word and by another land, / I'm bordered, if only a bit, by all things more and more."

In the immediate aftermath of the war Ingeborg Bachmann met a soldier in the British army, Jack Hamesh, who in 1938 had fled from Austria to find refuge in the Palestine Protectorate and now came to Carinthia with the Allies. From him, who was in love with her, she got a Jewish refugee's view of the Austria that had driven him into exile; she heard the tale, suppressed in Austria, of expulsion and extermination, and he for his part was astounded that in conquered Germany he had found a young woman who had read the books the Nazis burned.

In high-flown poetic tones she recorded in the *War Diary* this encounter, which epitomized for her the liberation from Hitler's tyranny and the hope for peace. "This is the loveliest summer of my life and if I live to be a hundred – this will still be the loveliest spring and summer ever" (Bachmann 2011, p. 23).

After the war Ingeborg Bachmann studied philosophy, first in Innsbruck and then in Graz. In the autumn of 1946 she went to Vienna and made contact there with the Viennese literary set. In May 1948 she encountered Paul Celan who, on his escape route from Bucharest, was spending six months in Vienna. At the end of June he set out for Paris. His Jewish parents had been deported from Czernowitz and murdered. When Ingeborg Bachmann met him, she was 22 years old and, crucially, he was six years her senior. In literary circles at the time he was regarded as the poetic counterpart to Franz Kafka. This was the start of a love affair the effects of which on her life and work can hardly be exaggerated. However, it is Celan's influence on her poetry that tends to be stressed. What gets overlooked is the fact that in the poems a dramatic dialogue unfolds in which she records her knowledge and recollection of his story and at the same time insists on it being different from her own story as a female writer. This process was made all the more painful by her awareness that her own father was a Nazi party member.

II

In the poems preceding her first volume of poetry, *Time on Loan – Poems 1948 to 1953*, Ingeborg Bachmann seems unaware of the challenge presented by Celan's work. Here the voice is still that of a disorientated lyrical self that has given in to "alienation" – "I can no longer see a path in any path" – and finds itself under a mythical spell: "Enchanted cloud mansion in which we drift" ("Without People"). It is only with the poems of *Time on Loan* (1953) that the self-addressed "you" can take stock, stand on its own two feet and go its own way.

"Outward Voyage" is the title of the first poem in this volume of verse. In the title poem too ("Time on Loan") Bachmann's resolute lines "Don't look round. Lace up your boot" are a call for action. What now seems called for is assertiveness: a commitment to her own story, to the words of the lover, to her own identity as a writer alongside that of Celan, the poet of the Shoah (Holocaust). The central stanza of "Time on Loan" begins with the lines "Out there your lover's engulfed in sand, / it climbs round her billowing hair, / it cuts short her words, / it tells her to be silent." "Out there" (Drüben) is the opening poem in Celan's first book of verse, *The Sand from the Urns*. The sand is Celan's code for the Shoah, the hair recalls the death-camps. Confronted with such calamitous experiences, the poet had to find a place for her own story and experiences if she was not to go under in silence. *Time on Loan* also signified awareness of a fresh start under threat from the Cold War and the resurgence of an old order, with time for change running out. The lively rhythmic gestures of the poems in this first book of verse, the calls and commands addressed to a second person, the warnings and exhortations, all relate to a precarious historical moment poised between "not yet" and "never again." The lyrical first person cannot accept that the great post-1945 hope, like others before it, may be at an end.

In the second book of verse, *Invocation of the Great Bear* (1956), the perspective of the poetic ego undergoes further change. The historical overview disappears to make way for an extension and demarcation of the self. Suppressed recollections of childhood start to have their say ("The Game is Up"). In a long poem, "About a Land, Its River and its Lakes," personal experience of life is mirrored in a landscape setting. The land is Carinthia with its profusion of lakes, the river is the Gail. But in these poems it is, above all, the experience of love that serves to define the self. *Invocation of the Great Bear* contains the most beautiful love poems in Bachmann's verse.

Ingeborg Bachman had moved to Italy in the summer of 1953, first to the Island of Ischia, then to Rome. In a letter from the end of July 1957 she writes about these first years in Italy, to which the poems of *Invocation of the Great Bear* belong, that it was then she "learned to trust her five senses" and became captivated by this new way of life with its insights and openness (Döpke 1994, p. 39). This new way of looking at things, as the celebrated Italy poem "The First Born Land" makes clear, had to be fought for. Like everything else in her work it was only to be won by putting her inmost being at stake, whatever the risk to her own life, so as to find in herself the power of redemption: "And as I drank myself / and earth tremors rocked / my first-born land, / I woke up clear-sighted." Her experience of the Italian landscape and the Mediterranean cult of festivities does not figure anywhere else as largely as in *Invocation of the Great Bear*.

III

Ingeborg Bachmann stayed in Italy from the summer of 1953 to the autumn of 1957, mostly in Rome. In the autumn of 1957 she moved to Munich. She met Max Frisch and in the autumn of 1958 moved to Zurich to be with him. Later the two of them lived by turns in Zurich and in Rome. At this time (1959-1960) she gave lectures in Frankfurt on Problems of Contemporary Poetry and produced her first volume of stories, *The Thirtieth Year*. After the break with Max Frisch and in the throes of a severe mental crisis she went to Berlin in 1963, staying there till the end of 1965. She returned to Rome to work on Kinds of Death, her projected cycle of novels, of which only one, *Malina* (1971), appeared in her lifetime. In 1972 she produced *Simultan*, a collection of stories. On 17 October 1973, at the age of 47, she died from burns sustained in a tragic fire accident at her flat in Rome.

From the end of the nineteen-fifties she regarded herself as a prose-writer and proclaimed more and more demonstratively this change of genre, in spite of the fact that literary criticism was increasingly focused on her poetry. In fact, even after the appearance of the second volume of poetry, she went on writing verse, as is clear from the collection presented here. Her most beautiful poems derived from a journey to Prague which she undertook, starting from Berlin, in January 1964, the date given in the title of one of these poems ("Prague January 64"). "Bohemia Lies on Sea," her homage to the poet of *The Winter's Tale* in the Shakespeare Year of 1964, also harks back to this journey. In her "Bohemian" poem we find the wishful dream of a peaceful world of minor figures and outsiders, the poor and the exiled. She called them Bohemians and illustrated them with figures from Shakespeare's comedies, while Bohemia itself was turned into a Utopian land on her "magic map," as she described it, of literature.

IV

Ingeborg Bachmann and Paul Celan are reckoned to be the most significant poets of post-1945 German-language literature. To this day Bachmann's poems have lost none of the power felt by her first readers in the early nineteen-fifties. In a letter of 15 May 1954 her close friend, the composer

Hans Werner Henze, wrote that he found in her poems "something alarming, scandalous, bewildering, startling" (Ingeborg Bachman/Hans Werner Henze 2004, p. 35). Almost 50 years later Ursula Höpfner, who was involved in a Bachmann production at Vienna's Burg Theater, said that the poetry could strike "quite suddenly into your very heart" and that "this is so terrifying, as if the world is coming to an end. She had courage and a good sense of humor and yet there was something childlike about her, but what stands out is the pain she feels for people and her sense of the forces shaping the relationships between men and women. Yet behind it all you feel an immense longing for love" (Höller 1999, p. 160 and f.).

The far-reaching influence of her verse is apparent in the work of contemporary writers, for instance, in Erich Fried's very personal biographical essay "On Ingeborg Bachmann's Bohemia Poem" (Fried 1983). Then there is Christa Wolf's interpretation of "Explain to me, Love" in the *Kassandra* lectures (Wolf 1983, p. 127 ff.) or Thomas Bernhard's tribute to her poems in his last novel, *Extinction* (Bernhard 1986, pp. 511 ff.). There her poems are placed on a par with those of Goethe while "Bohemia Lies on Sea" is described as "the best and finest poem ever to come from the pen of a female poet writing in German." In *Extinction* the narrator finds a memorable definition of what makes her poems special when he says that he has "always loved them because they are Austrian but, like no others, at the same time so utterly permeated with the world in its entirety and with everything around it."

The idea of these poems being both Austrian and open to the world reflects Bachmann's rejection of any specific regionalism. Here Bernhard has perhaps in mind Goethe's concept of a world literature, and with "Bohemian" he brings into play the Habsburg monarchy's landscape of memory, which never stopped being a source of inspiration in her work. Those Austrians who escaped after 1945 from the Nazi occupation sensed in Bachmann's work a closeness to the language of Viennese Modernism. Jean Améry, the great writer in exile, recognized the attraction he felt for Bachmann's language, the irresistible "magic" of the world of yesterday reaching out strangely into the world of today from which she couldn't escape (Améry 1972). Indeed, Musil, Rilke, Hofmannstahl, and first and foremost the philosopher Ludwig Wittgenstein all belonged to a tradition into which she felt drawn, yet of course without being totally seduced.

The huge influence of Bachmann's poetry and the high regard in which it is held is apparent in the numerous settings of her poems to music. The compositions of Hans Werner Henze take pride of place. In *Night Pieces and Arias* (1957) we find Bachmann's "In the Deluge of Roses" and "Safe Conduct" set to music as *Arias 1* and *2*. *Songs from an Island* was the name given by the composer to his *Choral Fantasies on Poems by Ingeborg Bachmann* (1967). The artistic collaboration with the world-famous German composer goes back to the early fifties. Her opera libretti are a product of his wish for collaboration, likewise the essay "Music and Poetry," which has as its aim the Utopian unification of the two sister arts. A pupil of Hans Werner Henze, Thomas Larcher, composed a new setting of "Bohemia Lies on Sea" (first performed in 2009), the product of an ambitious endeavor to transpose into music the Utopia of a Bachmann poem.

The influence of Bachmann's poems on the plastic arts, as demonstrated in the work of Anselm Kiefer, is unusual. His *Bachmann-Pictures* are all the more remarkable, given that since 1945 very few artistic works have attracted as much attention as his. One of these pictures, featuring lines from "The Game is Up," is displayed in a specially constructed pavilion opposite the Salzburg Festival Hall. Another one has the title *Bohemia Lies on Sea* and recalls with its monumental proportions Picasso's *Guernica*. There are no people in the picture; with Kiefer the intimation of an underlying warlike force comes from the "Bohemian" landscape and it is only "on the skyline" of one of her literary heartlands that the state of war becomes "visible," "something alarming, startling...."

V

Already in the 1956 collection, *Invocation of the Great Bear*, the opposite extremes of violence and love, war and peace had stood out with crystal clarity. Thematically the contrast is present in the tension between the grim foreboding of the title poem "Invocation of the Great Bear" and the hymn-like exaltation of "To the Sun" in lines such as: "Fair sun which, rising, has been mindful of its task / and ended it ...," "Fair light that keeps us warm, preserves us with marvelous care," or "Nothing more fair under the sun than to be under the sun...." Bachmann's song to the sun is her challenging riposte to the "Great Bear," to the constellation which for her embodies all the darkness and terror in the world, the violence of history represented in the nineteen-fifties by the atomic threat.

"Safe Conduct," which appeared a year after *Invocation of the Great Bear*, likewise fits into the context of the world-wide peace movement in the fifties. Hans Werner Henze described this poem against atomic annihilation as "one of the finest ever written" (Bachmann/Henze 2004, p. 161). It responds to the threat of atomic annihilation by demanding safe conduct for the earth and uses emotionally charged imagery to promote the notion of a new solidarity between man and nature.

In her final great interview with Gerda Haller, three months before her death, Bachmann made the link between her writing and the Utopia of peace: "This is something I deeply believe in and it is what I refer to as 'A day will come'.... It won't come and none the less I believe in it. For if I stop believing in it I cannot write any more" (Bachmann 2006, p. 34). This "A day will come" reflects the Utopia in "Bohemia Lies on Sea," which she reckoned to be her finest poem. It had been wrested from a world of war, the destructiveness of which is attested to in the texts of *I Know No Better World* (2000). Reading these texts one understands the sheer calamitous power of the experiences with which her Utopia of beauty had to contend.

The volume of poetry presented here comprises a representative selection of poems from every phase of the poet's output. The sequence is essentially chronological though it should be noted that the poems of *I Know No Better World* and *Miscellaneous Poems* actually date back to the period 1962-1964. Unprinted at the time, they lay in the family archive until recovered and published by the poet's literary executors, Heinz and Isolde Bachmann.

Hans Höller
Professor of Modern German
University of Salzburg

Translated by Mike Lyons

BIBLIOGRAPHY

Améry, Jean: "Trotta kehrt zurück." In: *Die Weltwoche* 41, 8 November 1972.

Bachmann, Ingeborg/Hans Werner Henze: *Briefe einer Freundschaft.* Hrg. v. Hans Höller. Mit einem Vorwort von Hans Werner Henze. München, Zürich: Piper, 2004.

Bachmann, Ingeborg: *Kriegstagebuch.* Mit Briefen von Jack Hamesh. Hrg. u. mit einem Nachwort von Hans Höller, Frankfurt am Main: Suhrkamp, 2011.

Bachmann, Ingeborg. *Wir müssen wahre Sätze finden. Gespräche und Interviews.* Hrg. Christine Koschel und Inge von Weidenbaum. München: Piper, 1983.

Bernhard, Thomas: *Auslöschung. Ein Zerfall.* Frankfurt am Main: Suhrkamp, 1986.

Döpke, Oswald: "Ich weiss nämlich gar nicht, wohin ich gehen soll." Ingeborg Bachmann in Briefen aus den Jahren 1956 und 1957. In: *du.* Heft Nr. 9, September 1994, pp. 36-39.

Fried, Erich: "Zu Ingeborg Bachmanns Böhmen-Gedicht." In: E. Fried: *Ich grenz noch an ein Wort und an ein andres Land.* Über Ingeborg Bachmann – Erinnerung, einige Anmerkungen zu ihrem Gedicht "Böhmen liegt am Meer" und ein Nachruf. Berlin: Friedenauer Presse, 1983, pp. 5-10.

Höller, Hans: *Ingeborg Bachmann.* Reinbek bei Hamburg: Rowohlt, 1999.

Larcati Arturo, Isolde Schiffermüller (Hrg.): *Ingeborg Bachmanns Gedichte aus dem Nachlass.* Eine kritische Bilanz. Darmstadt: Wissenschaftliche Buchgesellschaft, 2010.

Wolf, Christa: *Kassandra.* Voraussetzungen einer Erzählung. Neuwied: Luchterhand, 1983.